Eight Crayons

Polly —
Maybe there's a
Pastor's Column "starter"
or two here! I really
miss the 'old days'
in the Church office!

love,

John

July 5, 2011

OTHER BOOKS BY THE AUTHOR

Who Gets the Yellow Bananas?
Peter E. Randall, Publisher—2000

Breakfast in the Bathtub—A Book of Smiles
Co-authored with Fred Samuels
Peter E. Randall, Publisher—2005

Eight Crayons

Poems and Stories

by an *almost* sane woman

Joann Snow Duncanson

This book was printed in the United States of America.

Cover illustration and all art work by Melody Fellows
Copy editing by Trudie Bergeron
Author's photo by Heidi Duncanson

To order additional copies of this book, contact:
Xlibris Corporation
1-888-795-4274
www.Xlibris.com
Orders@Xlibris.com
97463

Contents

IV. A LITTLE MUSIC—A LITTLE FOOD

V. A RELATIONSHIP

VI. FAMILY MATTERS

VII. JUST FOR FUN

VIII. ON THE SERIOUS SIDE

IX. A POSTSCRIPT FOR POETS

This book is dedicated
to
the memory of Fred Samuels,
without whom my poetry might never
have seen the light of day,

and

to
RJ and Joey Duncanson
and
Andrew and Hope Weaver—
four shining stars
I am proud to call my grandchildren.

Acknowledgments

The following poems have been published previously:

"Summer on the Green"—*The 2010 Poet's Guide to New Hampshire*;

"The Whistler," "Invisible," "Eight Crayons," "Livin' in the Key of C," "Oatmeal in July"—*The Poet's Touchstone* (The Poetry Society of NH);

"Lower Me Gently"—*Currents* (The Seacoast Writers Association);

"Recycling, Anyone?," "I'm in Love with an Egg Salad Sandwich," "Summer on the Green," "The Whistler"—*The Greenland Grapevine;*

"Eight Crayons"—*The Portsmouth Herald*;

"Envy," "Rolling Home"—*Breakfast in the Bathtub;*

"The Walls of Rye"—*Rye Reflections.com*;

"Mothers Reflected"—*Who Gets the Yellow Bananas?*;

"Two Mothers"—*Embrace the Day* by Joanne Scherf; *The Angel Hearts Org.; Spark of Life Newsletter; DementiaCare of Australia; The Ribbon.com; Ellen Bailey Poems.com*. This poem has also been published by hospice and Alzheimer Associations in several countries, and in various newspaper obituaries.

All of the stories in this book have appeared previously in *the Peterborough Transcript* and/or *the Monadnock Ledger-Transcript*, Peterborough, NH.

Eight Crayons

If, as some say,
beginning a new year
is like opening a
brand new box of crayons,
then I wish for

five yellows
            for coloring the sun

two reds
            for coloring the heart

and just
one blue
            for those sad days
            when I don't feel like coloring
            at all.

I. People

The Whistler

—For Michael O'Neil

The little guy in the church pew
just behind me
is learning to whistle.
There's no mistaking it.

When the choir stops singing,
the organ cools down
and the minister
pauses mid-scripture,
I hear the small, breathy sound
that can only come
from the puckered lips of a
determined five-year-old boy,
faithfully practicing
his newfound skill,
fearing he might forget
how to do it.

And I sit here smiling
saying to myself:
you keep at it, little guy,
because some things in life
are worth striving for,
and one of them just
happens to be—*whistling!*

Mall Jewelry Girl

So many gold necklaces,
so many diamond rings,
so few customers.

I observe the pretty young clerk
standing behind her counter,
gazing wistfully at the paltry trickle
of mall shoppers passing by.
She's dressed perfectly for the part—
dark tailored suit,
hair pulled back into
a tight knot at the nape of her neck,
and, of course,
wearing a dazzlingly
beautiful necklace
with priceless earrings to match.
All this, yet not one would-be
customer entering the shop.

I can't help wondering, Jewelry Girl,
what will encircle that milky white neck
and what will dangle from those
soft, pink earlobes once five o'clock comes
and you head for your old, beat-up,
used Ford out in that parking lot?

Times are not good at the mall.
Times are not good anywhere.
Times are not good for a jewelry girl.

The Day Dorinda Came to the Poetry Society Meeting

I'll never forget the day
Dorinda came to the Poetry Society meeting.
As if swept through that door by the Muse itself,
in she wafted—fresh-faced, much younger
than the others gathered there.
She quickly took a seat near the front
then—suddenly—popped her woolen cap
straight up off her head
and out flew that vibrant red hair,
the shade of which most of us had never seen before—
a wondrous Kodak moment in the midst of what
could have been an otherwise monochromatic meeting.

Later, at announcement time, all heads turned
to our new young poet as she raised her hand to speak.
"My name is Dorinda. I've come to tell you about
the new and exciting cigarette machine poetry project!"
Now the members—some curious and others doubtful—
straightened in their chairs.

"We can recycle those old unused cigarette machines
into poetry machines," she said. "We'll merely type
up some poems on small sheets of paper,
roll them into cigarette shapes,
and fill the machines with them.
Soon, people will be dropping their coins
into the slots and buying our poems!"

Her enthusiasm was palpable, and after some discussion—
with members teetering between excitement and skepticism
and a few even volunteering to take part—the meeting ended.

I am sad to report that the cigarette machine project
was short-lived. It seems the transition from
nicotine to Neruda proved too difficult to survive.
As for Dorinda, we haven't seen her since.
Perhaps you know her, and if you do, please
tell her for me
that some of us will never forget the day
Dorinda came to the Poetry Society meeting.

At the Checkout Counter

Eileen has no intention of quitting her job
down at the A&P.
At 84, she drags my items across the checkout counter—
hands now knobby and stiff,
face lined deeply from years of living,
chin dotted with a few wiry, determined hairs.
"Nope, they'll have to carry me out feet first," she says,
as she pulls my groceries over the scanner.
Drag, scan, and push.

"Did pretty well at Bingo last week."
Her blue eyes take on a bright sparkle.
"Goin' down to the casino pretty soon!"
There is a slight hesitation at the checkout counter
as the world—and my groceries—pause to pay homage
to her other love, the gambling life.
Drag, scan, and push.

Finally, reminiscent of a sea captain
scanning the horizon in search of land,
she raises her right hand to shade her squinted eyes
in order to decipher the readout on the computer screen.
"$43.88," she declares.

Eileen has no intention of quitting her job
down at the A&P,
and I smile as I leave the store
and hear her asking the next customer the magic question . . .
"Paper or plastic?"

Catherine

—For Attorney Catherine Sage

Her hems swept the face of the sidewalk
as she moved through the streets of the town
like a broom gently brushing the pavement
in a dance—back and forth, up and down.

There she goes, there goes Catherine, we'd whisper,
part in mockery, yet mostly in awe,
for here walked the Maid of the Village—
a lady of stature and law.

She kept to herself, of her choosing,
and lived in a house filled with cats
that scampered all over the downtown
in search of fleet rodents and bats.

Though we're still perplexed by this lady
so silver-tongued, yet prone to cuss,
perhaps the more relevant question
is, *what did Ms. Sage think of us?*

Billy Collins—In the Palm of His Hand

He had us in the palm of his hand
even before he reached the podium that night,
before he settled his books and papers,
and certainly by the time he raised the pitcher
to pour water into that tiny paper cup.

Tiny paper cup?

Here was Billy Collins—former U.S. Poet Laureate,
knighted by Washington's Library of Congress
and sent out across this great land
to deliver simile and metaphor
to the literary washed and unwashed,
a living symbol of the very best in his trade—
and we offer him *a tiny paper cup*?

But wait!
Perhaps there is no need for Waterford crystal here
because Billy Collins—
this master at giving weight to whimsy
and whimsy to weight—
is a paper-cup poet. He says so himself
when he invites us into his poems
to dance with his words. He says so himself
when he appears on stage
in his casual sweater and open-collared shirt,
and gives us that smile.

Our evening with Billy Collins ended too soon,
and to the very last line of his very last poem,
he had us in the palm of his hand.
Then, in an appreciative yet unassuming way,
he simply gathered up his books and papers,
left the stage, and was gone.

And all that remained
was a half-full pitcher of water
and
a tiny paper cup.

Harold and Maude

At eighty-something, you'd see them down at the diner
sitting on the same side of the booth, still holding hands—
Maude, talking and talking,
and Harold, listening and listening—
a relationship skill learned early in this man's marriage.

Then, one quiet day they leave town—move up north
to one of those retirement places, and it happens—
Harold passes away suddenly,
leaving behind his devoted Maude—the love of his life
for over sixty years. How would she ever survive?

A scant few weeks pass—my phone rings—
it's Maude.
What can I say to this newly widowed woman?
How can I possibly ease her pain?

Then, rushing through the earpiece of my phone,
comes the breathless voice of a sixteen-year-old girl
emanating from the body of an obviously
no longer grief-stricken octogenarian:
"I've just met the most WONDERFUL MAN!"
exclaims Maude.

It appears that her wedding vow—
"until death do us part"—needs an addendum.
Perhaps these words,
"*. . . and not one moment longer,*"
would suffice.

Edna Wore Laughter

—For Edna Randall

Edna wore laughter
as one would a favorite sweater or coat.
She put it on every morning,
buttoned it up,
smoothed it down,
admired it in the mirror,
and set out on her daily rounds.

Edna wore laughter
no matter what the night before held
or the day ahead promised.
She wore it for others
to ease their souls.
She wore it for herself
to lessen her cancer pain.

Edna wore laughter—
hearty,
deep throated,
wonderful laughter—
until it magically became
a welcome,
treasured,
hand-me-down
for us all.

Charlene

"I'm never going to live in one of those!"
That's what Fred would say
at the mention of the term *nursing home.*
Little did he dream that by coming
to this place he would find not only
a very nurturing abode,
but he would find Charlene.

From the time he arrived,
and a beautiful young nursing assistant
named Charlene came to settle him in—
putting his clothes in drawers and closet,
saying reassuring things—
Fred was smitten.

It was her smile that captivated him first.
Fred was a pushover for a pretty girl.
Having eighty long years behind him
didn't change that one bit.

But he was not always easy to please—
after all, this former professor and poet
was caught in a long downward spiral
since the car accident,
and the road ahead looked grim,
but Charlene smiled on.
She would be there to get him up in the morning,
and always stopped by at the end of her shift
asking, "Can I do anything for you
before I go home?"

Then with that sweet smile, she'd add,
"I'll be here in the morning
to get you up and ready!"
Fred always knew her schedule—
she was his lifeline to the end.
Fred and Charlene—they were quite a pair.

Now someone new has moved
into Room 207—and hopefully,
a beautiful, smiling nursing assistant
has already appeared at their door saying,
"Good morning, my name is Charlene."

Doris Hadley, Where are You?

I don't know who Doris Hadley is or was—all I know is that this is the time of year I get her wonderful sweater out of the closet for its cold-weather outing. I'm sure she made this sweater because the label inside says, "From the knitting needles of Doris Hadley." That should be proof enough, although there is always the outside chance that Doris Hadley is a trade name. Looking at the workmanship, however, I doubt it.

Our sweater—Doris' and mine—is a heavy, white, fisherman knit cardigan. They're a challenge to make, with so many intricate configurations in the pattern. I suppose my friend Anne Hennessy who owns the Wool Room in Antrim, NH, could whip up one of these sweaters with relative ease, but novices like myself know when we've met our knitting-directions match.

I've knitted a few things in my day, but not all were successes. I made a tennis sweater for my husband once, only to discover when it was done that the sleeves came down below his knees. You can bet that wasn't a hit. Then there was the blue bouclé tie I knit for an old beau. It looked great when the date started out, but it had pretty much rolled up into a ball beneath his chin by the end of the evening. No, I stick with easy patterns these days, and leave the more intricate work to the Doris Hadleys and Anne Hennessys of this world.

I haven't a clue as to just when or where it was that Doris and I became a duo. All I know is, it was my lucky shopping day—just think, a beautiful woolen fisherman knit sweater for ten dollars.

Of course, when I got it home I realized that it was not made of wool at all, but acrylic—a synthetic yarn frowned upon by real knitters who knit only with a medium which once kept sheep warm. Yet if Doris wasn't a real knitter, I don't know who could be, because she knew her knits and purls. And so what if the sweater's not wool—it's plenty warm enough for me.

When you are a secondhand wardrobe shopper as I am, you sometimes wonder just who owned these things in the first place, and where did they wear them? For instance, I'll bet my grey wool skirt went to work in an office, with maybe a navy blazer and a white blouse topping off the outfit.

And that hot pink blouse hanging in my closet? The one with those wild black designs scampering over it? I'll wager that little number did a bit of dancing and living it up in some posh night spot. Just imagine how bored this poor blouse must be, living with the likes of me and my unglamorous lifestyle.

Since the recycling of clothing is so popular today, questions about original owners abound. Last month the local church had a rummage sale, and as I helped lift garment after garment out of large boxes and trash bags, my curiosity went into overdrive. Who wore this stuff, and where did they go with it? How much did it cost? (The ladies at the sale were "giving away" this clothing for two dollars a bag.) So many unanswered questions and unknown stories come with clothing once worn by strangers.

I wonder what Doris Hadley's story is. Did she come from these parts? Or was she from away? Did she have any children and, if so, did she pass her knitting skills down to ensuing generations? Why did she get rid of this nice sweater, anyway? Did she need the money? Was she going through hard times? Maybe she sold it at a craft fair.

I may never know the answer to those questions, but every time I pull on that magical sweater and fasten it with those big round wooden buttons, I feel this strange, warm kinship with a woman I never even knew. Thank you, Doris Hadley, wherever you are.

II. Places

Our Town

—Peterborough, NH

It's waking now, this town of ours,
the shades rise with the sun
and lamps turn on past window panes—
another day's begun.
Light dances on the belfry clock
and skips from peak to peak.
Roy's Market down on Main Street
gets shelves stocked for the week.
A truck coughs as its motor starts,
and jars the morning's still;
the diner puts the coffee on,
then fires up the grill.
The baker on the road just south
is mixing yeast with dough,
where pumpernickel, wheat, and rye
will soon begin to grow.
A flag is raised, Hobbs' door unlocks,
the mountain's in gold gown,
as you and I prepare to greet
a new day in Our Town.

The Baker-Wright Garage

In Portsmouth's Market Square—
the city's showplace—
locals lick their lattes
while tourists view their vistas;
eyes searching out one more shop,
one more bit of history
before turning homeward,
without even knowing
they are missing the best of all—
the Baker-Wright Garage.

So close you could hit with a lug nut,
this living memorial to garages past
is a place where time stands still—
a secret—as modest as its owner,
yet every bit as authentic a slice of
city history as any stone monument,
restored manse, or glistening bridge span
in this port city.

Floors preserved in years of crank oil,
walls lined with old tools dressed in DNA
from generations of calloused hands,
shelves crammed with crumbling cardboard boxes
harboring parts for makes of vehicles
that are no longer among the living.
An honest-to-god grease pit
where the owner spends most of his days
as did his father and grandfather before him,
with hands grimy, neck strained from peering upward

as he diagnoses, then remedies,
ailing vehicles of every kind—treating them
as if they were his very own.
All this, while over in the Square,
our city's tourists once again
fold their Chamber of Commerce
Visitors' Guides, tuck away
their newfound memories,
and head for home—
never even knowing
they are missing the very best of all—
the Baker-Wright garage.

Cell Phones at the Library

The sign in the local library reads,
"No cell phone use in this NONFICTION wing,"
and I hear my mind saying,
sure, but I'll bet there's no such sign
over in the FICTION wing.
You know how THOSE readers are—
always looking for a good time,
light reading,
the kind you can scan and talk on
the cell phone at the same time?

Humph!
Well, who cares!
It's nice and quiet over here
in the Nonfiction wing.
And who'd want to live
with Danielle Steele
all the time, anyway?

Summer on the Green

—Greenland, NH

'Twas a summer Thursday evening
when the bell in the church steeple
rang out a mighty six o'clock
reminding Greenland's people
to hurry to the bandstand,
there was no time to delay
or else they'd miss the action—
there's a concert on today!

Then folks rushed from their houses
with all sorts of things in tow—
picnic baskets, folding chairs,
to set out in a row.
There were pillows for their comfort,
there was bug spray just in case,
there were sunglasses and Sox caps
to keep sunlight off the face.

Some came on bikes or skate boards,
some rode in SUVs,
some neighbors merely came on foot
and crossed Post Road with ease.
There were cell phones nicely turned off,
there were dogs on leashes seen;
some tiny tykes in strollers,
blankets too, from L.L. Bean.

At last the bandstand came alive
and as notes began to climb,
the wee ones danced their feet off
while the grandmas clapped in time.
An evening to remember—
a Norman Rockwell scene—
just folks from a New England town
sharing summer on the Green.

A Visit at Wallis Sands Beach

—Rye, NH

I had a visit with Millie today—
thought she might like some company.
She doesn't know me, and all I know of her
is what is written on the plaque affixed to her bench:
    "Millie McIntyre, 1920–1995,"
just enough to tell me that she loved this place—
probably spread her blanket and set up her favorite
beach chair here on this sand more times than
she could count.

She saw sand castles rise and fall with the tides,
countless holes dug by small hands wielding tiny shovels,
suntanned lovers sharing towels barely large enough for one—
a scene playing over and over again like a welcome,
never-ending encore for a favorite symphony.

Today Millie, Betsy Bacon, Paul and Claire Davis,
and the others, keep watch here from their
memorial benches lining the pathway between
the sod and sand—offering weary beach goers
a place to rest while collecting one more
seaside memory before starting for home.

Once our visit ended, I drove away from the beach
with some of the names on those benches still shining
in the rear view mirror of my mind—Albert Grande,
Thomas Bonano, Arthur and Esther Gray, Richard Lyons,
the Gaults . . .

The days are growing shorter now and winter will be coming on,
yet we have no need to worry about our treasured Wallis Sands.
Millie and her faithful friends will surely watch over
our seaside treasure, keeping it safe until we meet again.
After all, they loved this special place, too.

Epsom Circle Elegy

On a dark, rain-soaked morning in June
the State of New Hampshire
renamed the Epsom traffic circle,
honoring two brave police officers
gunned down in the line of duty.

Family members watched proudly
as the round patch of earth beneath
their feet was officially declared the
Jeremy Charron and Michael Briggs Circle.

How graciously they acknowledged this
public tribute for their loved ones,
yet deep down
they knew—
as we know—
you cannot welcome a traffic circle home
after a hard day's work,
or serve it a helping of favorite lasagna,
or call to remind it
to bring home the milk and bread,
or feel the familiar curve of its body
lying next to you night after night.

The sad truth is this:
you cannot hug a traffic circle.

The Walls of Rye

Stone on stone, they line the roads of Rye—
leading through the town and toward the sea—
leaving a bewildered you and I
to wonder how such treasures came to be.

Mile on mile they grace our country ride—
grey ribbons, warm in sunshine, cold in snow—
they cradle us with arms on either side,
yet whose hands built them, we may never know.

Like never-ending skeins of twisting yarn—
no telling where they stop or they begin—
they guard each spreading field, each house, each barn,
while keeping people out, or people in.

How fortunate for us that they still stand—
these cobbled hems that line our landscape's gown—
declaring their allegiance, stone to land,
grey brush strokes on the portrait of a town.

A Roy's Market Story—Almost!

I'd always wanted to write about Peterborough NH's Roy's Market. Thinking it would make a perfect subject to submit to Yankee Magazine, one day a few years ago I began working on an outline for such a piece. Then over coffee at the diner one morning I happened to mention to one of Roy's Market's employees that I was writing about his place of business.

"Oh, you'd better ask Mr. Roy first," was his comment. So when I reached a certain point in my story, I gathered up my "Roy's" folder and headed down to the store.

Florence—earnest faced, gentle, and quintessential New England—was at the register, busily processing a woman's groceries. No sign of any scanners here, of course. Instead, once she'd tallied up the amount, Florence wrote it on a tiny slip of paper, had the customer sign it, then that snippet of paper was put somewhere in the vicinity of the cash register until who knows when it got paid. No one at Roy's seemed to worry that those slips could fail to turn into real money some day.

"Is Mr. Roy here?" I asked Florence.

"Somewhere—you'd better ask Noel," she replied.

I proceeded toward what was generally known as the Nerve Center of the store—the meat department. Noel was one of three in red jackets, looking more like the head waiter at The Plaza than a man readying your Sunday rib roast. That touch of formality, by the way, was just one of Roy's secret charms.

At first I hesitated to ask Noel a question, for he was known for pulling the legs of more than just chickens. Like the time I hunted high and low for applesauce, and finally asked him whether they carried it. "Sure do," he said with a knowing smile, leaving me, of course, without a clue as to exactly where it was in the store. That was vintage Noel.

So on the day of my search for Mr. Roy, I bit the bullet and asked Noel where I could find him. "Down under the stairs," came the reply.

Hmmmm, I thought, as I headed down the old wooden stairs, *this should be interesting.* And sure enough, I found Mr. Roy directly under the turn in the stairway, reminiscent of a Charles Dickens character, going over the accounts. This at least gave me some assurance that those little slips of paper surely did get processed.

I explained that I was writing a piece about the store for submission to Yankee Magazine, and wanted his permission. After a few pleasantries, this very popular yet extremely private man told me he'd rather I didn't write about the store. He said he was sure I'd do a good job but he just didn't want any publicity.

Undaunted, I mentioned a few store features I would write about, and still the answer was no. After another attempt on my part to win him over, he said, "Well, I suppose it would be all right if you wrote it, (and then came the clincher) as long as you don't mention me."

As you can imagine, writing about a store named Roy's would be rather difficult without mentioning the man whose name it bore. So in respect for his quiet, modest, and unassuming ways, I thanked him for considering it, folded up my "Roy's" file, and climbed the stairs to daylight—passing Noel's familiar whistling in the meat department, and the clanging of the old cash register, with Florence nicely serving a line of very happy customers.

Now you know the story of why I never got to write about Roy's Market. Too bad, because it would have been a classic—Norman Rockwell, Thornton Wilder, and Shur-Fine groceries, all wrapped into one. By the way, Roy's Market is still there on Main Street. Check it out when you're in the area, but don't even *think* of writing about it. I tried.

III. Women's Issues

Invisible

I cannot recall the exact day
they stopped noticing me—
the moment I became invisible,
absorbed into the passing crowd
without the turning of a single male head.

Perhaps it happened slowly:
the rising of the years, the falling of the breasts,
the graying of the hair, the slowing of the step,
day—by month—by year.

We older women never forget what it was like
when young men actually saw us.
When, with one brief glance,
they took in the contours of our bodies,
the cadence of our step, the essence of our scent—
while we pretended not to see them at all.

So, just when did these men stop noticing us?
Perhaps a more relevant question is this:
when will *we* stop noticing *them*?

Checkup—Chin Up

The clinic receptionist
is checking me in—
asks for my insurance cards,
then my date of birth.
I tell her, and then
she stops her typing,
turns from her computer
and says,
"I'm trying to do the math here . . .
you simply can't be that age!"
I sit taller in my chair,
soaking up that compliment
like one big happy
postmenopausal sponge.

Later, on my way out, I notice
she is processing another woman
I hurry past her desk
so I won't have to hear her say,
"I'm trying to do the math here . . ."

Mastectomy

Madeline is losing one today.
For eighty-nine years, there were two,
as sure as there were two eyes
and ears and hands and feet
there were two of them.
Now they are taking one away.

Gloved tailors in green sterile masks
and gowns will cut, lift, and sew.
There will be no calling hours—
no burial rites for this soft mound
of diseased flesh.

But Madeline's body will grieve.
Oh, how it will grieve.

Oatmeal in July

The diner waitress, hair hanging limp
from the summer humidity,
sets the heavy bowl
with its hot steaming contents
on the counter, square in front of me.

The stoolmate on my right gulps down
a frosty bottle of Bud Lite,
as sweat pours down his neck and past the
straps of his "Bikers Make Great Lovers" tank top.

Loud, angry voices escape from the kitchen:
"Turn on the damned air conditioner!" shouts one—
"Open the window and get some fresh air!"
screams the other.

It is July—
and I stare down at my bowl of hot oatmeal,
cursing the chemotherapy
that makes my blood
run so cold.

The Second Round

He cautioned me not to get my hopes up.
After his late wife finished chemo
the doctor told her she had to start all over again—
as if ordering another round at the bar:
"Belly up to the Methotrexate, gals—
intravenous all around!"

I bleed for her;
but I weep for me, too.
Yesterday it was all over—
six long months of it—
the needles searching for my "best vein,"
the drawing of the blood,
nurses suiting up in spaceship masks,
coveralls, and bright purple gloves,
before they administered "it"—
the cocktail to zap my cancer.

Now, though out of caring,
he tells me
she had to go for a futile
second round.

Tomorrow I see my oncologist
for his report.
I tell myself I will be positive—
I tell myself I will be fine—
yet there will still be that small
warning voice in my head saying,
". . . but she had to go for a second round."

The Unveiling

I hesitated at first—
taking off my clothes
with him there, watching me.
No one had seen me this way—
not since the mastectomy.

I worried as he sat and stared,
steady eyes absorbing my nakedness—
the now incomplete landscape of my torso—
yet he made no move to leave.
It was then that I knew—
my cat cares little about symmetry.

Envy

The girl just ahead of me in the mall coffee shop line
is tall,
beautiful,
and of no more than eighteen summers.

My eyes cannot help focusing on her back,
obstructed only by the saucy strings of her
tomato-red halter top.
The landscape of her flesh is smooth
and flawless.

My own flesh, once clear and smooth to his touch,
and every bit as perfect as hers,
has now become a canvas where the paintbrush of age
has daubed and splashed designs of ugly moles,
and the faint renderings of meandering blue veins.

Just when I find myself on the brink of drowning
in a swirling eddy of self pity and youth envy,
the young girl reaches for her coffee cup,
causing her tomato-red strings to shift ever so slightly.
Just enough to reveal—yes, I see them—
two small but determined brown moles
near the nape of her neck.

I catch myself smiling as I utter under my breath,
"There *is* a God!"

Widows Don't Dance
at the Weddings

Widows don't dance at the weddings—
look at that one over there!
Half the reception is over and done
and she's never once moved from her chair.

She smiles as she watches the dancers
but her mind wanders far from this day,
remembering when it was *her* turn to wed
and *her* father gave *her* away.

Oh, as a young bride she was striking—
everyone there said the same.
She smiled at the young man who stood by her side
who was sharing his love and his name.
And they danced their first dance as a couple
while the guests crowded 'round on that floor.
They danced through the years they were married until
he was gone, and the dance was no more.

So she sits here today, never moving,
with her memories haunting her yet,
knowing widows don't dance at the weddings
for they've too many songs to forget.

Older Men—Younger Men

A woman should never wed an older man,
yet that's the way it's been since time began—
  despite tables actuarial
  and sad times so funereal,
older men still loom quite large in the bridal plan.

Now men, of course, like things just as they are—
choosing mates the way they might a brand new car—
  with mileage nice and low,
  and with such get-up-and-go,
a brand new model's bound to take them far.

Yet women are not dense; they know there's merit
in older men, so they just grin and bear it—
  for though *age-wise* men have passed them,
  these wives figure they'll outlast them
until someday all their savings they'll inherit.

A Mother's Gift

Former U.S. Poet Laureate Billy Collins once wrote a wonderful poem entitled "The Lanyard." It involved a camping experience, a young boy, his mother, and of course, a lanyard.

In the poem, he recalls his fledgling foray into the world of camp arts and crafts, and learning how to make a lanyard. Though not even sure what lanyards were, he somehow persevered and wove those colorful plastic strips back and forth until he ended up with a very special gift for his mother. When he returned home from camp, he proudly presented her with his handmade lanyard, and was certain this was one of the nicest gifts his mother would receive in her entire life.

Later in the poem, the grown-up Collins begins to examine the childhood audacity of the idea that this little plastic lanyard could have somehow repaid his mother for all the things she had done for him. He then lists them, including bringing him into the world, nursing him through illnesses, and serving him countless meals, etc. After each one of these realizations, and in a very proud voice, he'd brag that he gave his mother a lanyard. When Collins reads this to an audience, everyone smiles or laughs because they too realize that though well-meaning, that plastic lanyard had a long way to go to make up for the things his mother did for him.

Of course, most mothers have received these lovingly prepared handmade gifts over the years and have done so gladly. Each Christmas when our family gets out the decorations we find a few such gems. My favorite is a holiday wreath my children made by glueing pieces of macaroni onto a cardboard ring and spraying it with gold paint. Chances are, your family has at least one of these in the attic too. Although ours is a sorry sight now, with only three or four pieces of pasta clinging to it, what mother could throw out something made with the loving hands of her own children? Not yours truly, evidently.

And how about those prints made by little kindergarten hands dipped in red, yellow, and blue paint and affixed to shiny paper—remember those? Then there were those early family portraits where the pint-sized artists would invariably draw a mother much shorter than the siblings, or even the dog. These things are collectors' items.

Lasting gifts for mothers don't have to be expensive or even handmade. They can come in other ways: a phone call, an invitation, a photograph. For instance, when I was going through breast cancer treatment, my daughter was right there helping me. That was a gift that didn't cost money but it was priceless and paid me back in spades for any mothering I did for her. Now, since I live next door, she shares her entire family with me—another fantastic gift.

And then there was the letter from my son. In his mid-twenties and about to take his first plane trip to California (and I was leaving for England), he wanted to get some things down on paper before we both left. He thanked me for everything I had ever done for him, even for taking him to Boston for his first Bruins hockey and Celtics basketball games. He went on to say that even though I never really knew much about sports (and that was putting it mildly), he liked the fact that I jumped up and down with him in the family room when Doug Flutie threw his Hail Mary pass. The letter ended by saying he especially wanted to thank me for being both father and mother to him after his dad died. What a gift that letter was—and is today.

So there are all kinds of gifts we mothers receive from our children, and whether they are large or small, we treasure them—macaroni wreaths, scrawled family portraits, plastic lanyards and all.

IV. A Little Music--
A Little Food

Livin' in the Key of C

Sometimes you get tired of livin' in the Key of C.
You want to branch out a little—do something wild,
like quit your job,
chuck all your material belongings,
tattoo your buttocks.
Now, that would be living—
probably in the Key of F
or maybe even F Sharp.

Hanging out in C is too predictable:
your tomorrow is today, only with a different name.
Coffee in the morning, veggie wrap at noon, tea at four—
where's the fun in that?
All white keys. No black ones to tweak the melody.

Sometimes we slip a little and end up in B Minor—
a relationship fails, or a body part goes awry—
but soon we are right back where we started,
in the good old Key of C.

If there really is a god somewhere
in charge of things like these,
I want a fresh start—
a little less Strauss and a little more Stravinsky—
a brand new home on the scale of life.

I'd even settle for a D Minor.

Peggy Lee in Market Square

—Portsmouth, NH

Peggy Lee is singing her heart out
in Market Square.
Her sultry tones are wafting
over the laptops and lattes
of the busy young patrons
in the Breaking New Grounds café
and they don't even hear her—
they don't even know who she was.

> *"Is that all there is? Is that all there is . . ."*
> *"Lover, when I'm near you . . ."*
> *"Fever! You give me fever . . ."*

I sit back in my chair,
spread one more buttery yellow mound
across the last bite of a blueberry scone,
raise my cup of hazelnut decaf,
and smile.

I hear you, Peggy.
I hear you.

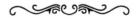

The No-Poem Blues

If you haven't got a poem in your pocket or your purse
or a jot or a tittle of a scintillating verse
and you're sitting at an open mic, well, what could be worse?
   You've got the old *No-Poem Blues!*

No matter how you've tweaked that brain in your head,
your rhymes aren't working and your metaphors are dead,
you're thinking that you should have stayed home instead
   with those nasty old *No-Poem Blues!*

What will you say there, what will you do?
Everybody else has a poem but you—
you could climb 'neath the table and hide in your shoe
   with your wicked old *No-Poem Blues!*

But when the thing's over and you're ready for flight,
someone comes along and makes it all right—
saying, "We surely did miss your poem tonight !"
   So long, old *No-Poem Blues!*

Day Lilies and Golden Jazz

Day,
by day,
by Day Lily,
these golden horns
announce each coming dawn.

No Armstrong,
Gillespie,
or
Marsalis
could make sweeter
yellow reveille
than this.

The Violinist

I noticed her the moment I took my seat.
How could anyone *not* notice her?

Hair the color of lemon sorbet,
flaming red dress with high mandarin collar,
demure slits teasing those
delicately crossed ankles?
She, the lone violinist on stage,
was every inch the professional—
pure elegance—
sitting with her back stick-straight
on the very edge of her chair,
waiting for the concert to begin.

Finally the lights dimmed,
the audience settled down,
the musicians took up their instruments,
the conductor raised his baton,

and then—

the Greenland Junior High School Jazz Band
commenced to blow, drum, and strum
its way through ear-piercing—yet spirited—renditions
of "Louie, Louie" and "The James Bond Theme."

And all the while, our violinist—
strings barely audible above the din—
played on.

How could anyone *not* notice her?

Ode to a Popover

You can share a tuna sandwich
or a tasty ham on rye
or a nice downtown apartment
or some other woman's guy,
but you cannot share a popover—
the palate's rarest find—
unless you've shed your taste buds
or completely lost your mind.

A popover's a treasure
to savor and adore
from its shiny, crusty roof top
to its luscious egg-y floor.
And sure, the thing looks frumpy
but it's been through such a lot,
starting life down in that muffin tin
as just a tiny spot.

So mind these words of wisdom
offered fervently and free:
you must *never* share a popover
unless it is—*with me!*

Hasta la Vista, Betty Crocker!

I'm throwing out the cookbooks—
the ones lining my kitchen counter for years
like dusty, culinary terra cotta warriors
once revered—no longer needed.

Do not look for lingering traces of flour
or any of my DNA on these pages—
their recipes still in virgin state,
untouched and undesired, at least by me.

But cooking is creative, you say,
and you are creative.
That is true, but the problem is this:
I cannot seem to coax my mind away
from frolicking in its idea-filled sandbox
long enough to do a thoughtless thing like
saute a shrimp, or puree a parsnip.

So, goodbye *Joy of Cooking!*
Farewell, *Martha Stewart!*
Hasta la vista, *Betty Crocker!*
I'm going out to lunch now.

I'm in Love with an Egg Salad Sandwich

—Greenland, NH

I'm in love with an egg salad sandwich—
I know it's absurd, but it's true—
and when saddled with such an addiction,
not just *any* egg salad will do.
I drive to our town's Suds N' Soda
more times than I'd care to admit,
and not for a Bud Lite or Pepsi
'cause for me that *egg sandwich* is it.

I rush to the place where they keep them
in a case near the back of the store
and hope that the shoppers before me
didn't beat me, and left me no more.
The lady who makes all these lunches
is a pro, and has just the right touch—
a little of this and a bit more of that,
and mayo? Just right, not too much.

Someday I am sure I'll outgrow this—
I'll move on to sliced ham on rye;
I'll quit my cholesterol habit—
give some of her chili a try.
But meanwhile I'm stuck with this problem
even therapists couldn't unwind—
I'm in love with an egg salad sandwich
but I can't say the same for my mind.

Bahs and Squayahs

A member of the ladies' circle
had just gone to her reward;
this day's meeting agenda
would deal primarily with food—
namely, which repast these women
should serve at the funeral reception
for their dear friend, the deceased.

"Casseroles!" suggests the lady in the
back, as she pauses mid-row in her knitting.
Then from a well-coifed, perfectly coordinated
woman in the front row comes, "Finger sandwiches—
people always like our finger sandwiches."

The room suddenly falls into two camps:
the casserole team versus the sandwich crowd,
until finally their leader rises to her feet
and in her sturdiest presidential voice declares:
"BAHS and SQUAYAHS—
we will provide bahs and squayahs."

I, a newcomer, and not privy
to local culinary terms do the unthinkable—
raise my hand and ask,
"Excuse me, just what are bahs and squayahs?"
The answer is swift and sure:
"You know," replies the president,
"like brownies."

I push the issue one step further.
"Is a brownie a bah or a squayah?"
Without batting an eye she replies,
"That depends on how you cut 'em.
If they're long and thin, they're a bah,
but if they are squayah . . ."
Where *is Fritz Wetherbee**
when you need him?

*Author: *Fritz Wetherbee's New Hampshire*

I Still Love You

I've loved you for such a long time—
what was I, twenty-one?
With so many dreams,
so little experience, while you—
you were the seasoned one—
sought after, well traveled,
name on so many lips,
yet I dared to love you.

And all those other women—
I'd watch as they reached out to you,
inhaling your scent, tasting your body,
and yet I still loved you.

The truth is this:
whether full-bodied or mild,
with cream or black,
decaf or regular,
instant or brewed,
in a mug or a china cup,
Starbucks or Sanka—
I still love you, coffee!
I still love you.

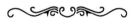

Down at Screamers Café

Somehow I have become a "regular" down at Screamers Café even though I don't quite fit their profile. Most of their patrons have ages in the single digits and go there to play while their moms relax and have coffee or lunch with other moms. It's a concept that owner Leslie Blaney came up with after she, her husband, and two young daughters moved to the town of Stratham, NH. On finding no eatery in the area casual enough to cater to both children and their parents, she decided to start one herself, and we regulars are glad she did.

I found the place one day when I was in need of a cup of coffee after my workout at a nearby gym, and though I quit that gym long ago, I can't seem to kick the Screamers habit. One reason for this is Leslie herself. She can be up to her elbows in cake batter, but will stop to greet you the minute you hit the door. She's also a fantastic cook who's not afraid to experiment now and then. We all gasped when she said she was going to start cooking classes for preschoolers. Well, guess what? Those pint-sized Rachael Rays have produced everything from meatloaf to pizza and from Chicken Cordon Bleu to Fettuccini Alfredo. Not bad for a bunch of little guys whose knowledge of entrees once began and ended with chicken nuggets and fries.

Screamers is a cross between two TV shows—*The View* and *Cheers*. *The View*, because the regulars love to talk, and no subject is off limits. And like the *Cheers* regulars, they've made the place a home away from home—while I may stop in two or three times a week, some of them are there two or three times a day. Screamers is addictive; it's therapy with food.

Most of these regulars are moms ranging from their twenties to forties, and even though I'm old enough to be their mother or grandmother, they somehow seem to accept me. They probably sense that I'm a bit on the offbeat side myself. Maybe that's why I got invited to their annual first-day-of-school bash. I'd already picked up rumors about it. "Don't forget Wednesday morning at 8:15!" said one. "As soon as that school bus pulls out, I'm heading down here," exclaimed another.

The next thing I knew they were talking about pajamas. They were all going to come in pajamas. With that, my mind flew to my nightwear inventory. I knew perfectly well that what I wore to bed and what these young women wore were two very different things.

The last hint about the upcoming gala came when someone mentioned that she was bringing "the stuff." What stuff, I wondered—surely Screamers was supplying the food.

At 8:10 on Wednesday morning I was in my car, dressed in a pair of old sweat pants and tee shirt (which I do sometimes wear to bed), and heading to Screamers.

I arrived to find some of them already there—a batch of moms who love their children, but don't mind celebrating their freedom once the school season cranks up for another year. And yes, they were in their pajamas. The one with big purple elephants printed all over hers said it was a hoot standing at the bus stop like that. "I'll bet the bus driver and all those kids took me for a Republican!" she laughed.

Leslie (not in pajamas) had the coffee on and served a great breakfast spread, complete with one of those party fountains spouting orange juice. Oh, and the stuff? Someone brought champagne to turn those glasses of orange juice into Mimosas.

When Screamers first opened, its focus was on ice cream, as in "I scream, you scream, we all scream for ice cream." Now it's evolved into a place where little ones come to eat, play, and yes, sometimes scream. But it's also a place where one morning a year a collection of fun-loving, pajama-clad moms celebrate their first-day-of-school freedom. Where else, but down at Screamers Café.

V. A Relationship

Seven Days

I measure my life in increments of seven days.
Like a seamstress, I place my pins into the metered fabric of my life;
always equidistant, always precise.

In seven days I will get into my car, drive away from the sun
toward a light in human form; he will shine in his doorway.

In seven days I will shed my life here, for one there.
My cat for his cat.
My sofa for his sofa.
My bed for his bed.

In seven days we will come together,
three score and ten times two—
grey beard against drying cheek,
wedding ring-less hands touching.
Poet/Prose Maker.
Jew/Christian.
Man/Woman.

In seven days we will share our songs
and speak
of yesterday
and how it shaped us—
of today
and what we have become.
We never speak of long tomorrows.

On the eighth day I will turn my car back toward
the setting sun,
my skin still feeling the warmth of the other light
shining in the rear view mirror of my mind.
I will pass a point on the road where for a single moment
these two nourishing orbs become one,

and then—

I will feel the familiar pull of home,
where once again
I will measure my life in increments of seven days—
my seamstress fingers straining to place
each pin closer to the next.

Cranberries in Snow

Looking out his bedroom window
I see that snow has fallen in the night,
dusting the high cranberry bush,
now grown tall as the eaves of the old red house.

It is October, and the impatient flakes,
not willing to wait until their time,
have dressed each crimson berry
in a white crystalline bonnet—
a rare still life
framed by the frost-edged window.

As I savor the beauty of it all
I find myself thinking of his late wife.
Did she ever look out this window at such a sight;
did she ever get to see the cranberries in snow?
Did they help to warm her spirits—
or cool her cancer pain?

The morning sun begins to warm the berries,
and as the snow melts from each one,
I come to realize
that the more I know him,
the more I am drawn to her.

Then suddenly I sense
that there are three of us in the room—
and I smile.

Beach Vigil

I follow his gaze across the sand to her;
  —she is lithe,
  —she is beautiful,
  —she is young.

She catches my attention, too,
wrapping me in a dark quilt of envy,
reminding me of my own youth:
  —before cellulite,
  —before sagging breasts,
  —before the kid in McDonald's
    started asking the 'senior' question.

I glance back at him, grey beard glinting in the sun,
and I wonder if he grieves for his old life, too:
  —before receding hairline,
  —before growing prostate,
  —before the waitresses began calling him Sweetie?

Suddenly the young woman rises from her seaside perch,
shakes her flowing hair and sandy towel,
and strides away, down the beach.

As I watch her slim outline fade into the afternoon sun,
my body eases back into the warm contours of my chair—
but my mind wonders how long it will be
before the next one comes along.

Late Harvest—Late Love

Our earlier plantings came up pretty much on time.
Eagerly anticipated, they didn't disappoint us;
those young marriages delighting our eyes
and nourishing our bodies
far beyond, perhaps, what we dared to expect.

As May turned to June, and June welcomed July,
we grew in their warmth and their selflessness.
Our lives took on predictable, comfortable rhythms.

Then suddenly, well before summer's end,
they were gone.
Partners called back—
their seasons cut much too short—
and we wrapped ourselves in grey mourning pain.

After a time—and quite unexpectedly—
new shoots appeared.

A late harvest—a late love.

Not as vigorous as the first—
flesh less perfect, color less bright—
yet so welcome a gift for each of our lives.

Now we savor these autumn days together—
this nourishing reprieve—
as we quietly turn the calendar,
with its warnings of inevitable cold,
toward an eyeless wall.

Now the Dreams Come

Now that he is gone,
the dreams come—
nocturnal visits
pulling me back.

He seems younger
somehow—
relaxed, smiling,
almost carefree.

I, too, am there—
fairer of face
and dressed in a more
compassionate gown.

Perhaps that is the way
it was supposed to be
all along.

My Friend Fred

My friend Fred and I never did see eye-to-eye on everything. Take the Big Bang theory for instance. His view was that anyone with half a brain knew that the world couldn't possibly have begun from an infinitesimal speck, no matter what the scientists tell you. Besides, he'd say, where did they think the speck came from in the first place? According to him, too many weak-minded people were just going along with those scientists because of their professional credentials. Fred seemed to have had it in for scientists.

Arguing with Fred wasn't easy. For one thing, he was a retired professor with a Ph.D., while I admit to having run gleefully from the halls of academia, B.A. degree in hand, never to return.

For another thing, I didn't come down on either the scientific or biblical side of how the world began, and this drove Fred to distraction. He'd much rather that I'd jump to the defense of the scientists so he could expound against them, but I didn't have a clue as to how this world began and I doubted that I'd have a definitive answer in my lifetime. You'd think our nonargument would have died then and there, but Fred couldn't let go of it. We wrestled with this topic off and on for the whole ten years I knew him.

I say "knew" because Fred died recently, and not by the most natural of causes, unless you call skidding off the road during an ice storm natural. After suffering a few freezing nights in his powerless home in the New Hampshire woods, he decided to check in at a nearby Inn to wait out the power outage. The next morning, however, he got worrying about the birds he fed each day, and those raccoons that came to his back porch every evening for their fill of dry cat food, so he drove back home to feed them all. It was on his return trip to the Inn that his car skidded on ice and into a tree, thus triggering a list of health problems that led to his demise.

Fred was one of those individuals who tweaked your conscience because he lived the "right" way. He never met a vegetable he didn't like and would salivate over the taste of steamed Swiss chard the way I would over a hot fudge sundae. And if you wanted sugar in your tea at his house, just forget it. He began every day with his Tai Chi routine plus an aerobic walk down his country road, wrote his poetry, and fed those birds and raccoons. In other words, Fred lived as peaceful and healthful a life as a 79-year-old man could—until he hit that patch of ice.

When you lose a close friend like Fred, it takes a while to realize the many ways your routine has changed and the things you miss. For instance, this morning I opened the paper to check the horoscopes. Fred and I often phoned each other to joke about how our predestined days were to unfold. Now I merely check my Aries section and leave Capricorn to the December and January people.

Then there was baseball. Though born and raised in Brooklyn, Fred was a big Red Sox fan. When I met him I was barely able to distinguish between a ball and a strike, but now, thanks to him, I know about splitters and ground rule doubles, and that there's a psychology to the game. Now when I watch a Sox game, I cheer loudly from my recliner for both of us.

Fred also taught me that all living things have beauty and worth, so if a few patches of goldenrod or dandelions take root in your lawn, so what? And those spindly-legged spiders in the tub? Why not carefully escort them out the door to live another day? Fred did.

I miss Fred, and in a strange kind of way, I even miss our arguments. Maybe if he'd lived a few years longer, he'd have won me over to his view of the Big Bang theory.

Well, perhaps.

VI. Family Matters

Stretching Out

My sister called the other day.
It seems she's decided against cremation—
says she wants to be able to stretch out.

Sometimes last wishes are so weird.

My Mother's Name

My mother never liked the name Hazel—
said she never knew a pretty one.
Her middle name, Mae,
didn't please her that much either
but she made it through life just the same,
carrying both names along with her
like a set of luggage received as an unwanted gift
from distant relatives who didn't know her taste.

My mother worked in a hotel kitchen—
arms bearing red scars of reaching too many times
into those too-hot ovens. Coming home
in late afternoons, shedding symbols of her day
from front door to bedroom.
First the well-worn work shoes
with sides slit open to ease the bunion pain.
Next the stockings, then further down the hall, the girdle—
a metaphoric trail of a hard day's work.

My mother was a loner, forced only by convention
to join an occasional group, never quite recovering
from having to march in parades with the American Legion Auxiliary
or withstand the ritual of the Eastern Star ladies' meetings—
obligations in her marriage she'd never have chosen for herself.

My mother was never offered a sterling silver dessert tray
stacked high with life's best opportunities,
but I will tell you this—
she could sing like a bird, play a mean piano,
cook like the greatest chefs in the finest hotels,
and match wits with the best of them.

Not bad for a woman
welcomed into this world
with the name
Hazel Mae.

Keeping Watch

I've watched them go before—the minds—
first grandmother, then mother.
Thoughts once sharp and focused,
then struggling with blankets of fog
wrapped so tightly around their brains.
that they no longer saw me—
worse yet, I no longer saw them.

Then I watch my friends—
as the clock ticks longer and louder,
they haltingly try to make withdrawals
from the safe deposit boxes of
their aging minds.
Elusive words,
and once familiar names
all come slowly now,
followed by nervous quips
about "Senior Moments,"
and that reassuring phrase—
"We all do it."

Finally, I turn the microscope inward
to the most painful vigil of all—
and I watch and worry
as those dreaded fingers of fog
begin tightening around
my own waiting brain
until even I
no longer know
who
I
am.

Father, Does it Matter?

I don't even know for sure that you were my father.
My real father. The one with the seed.
The one who slept with my mother
eight years after the last of the others was born—
nine months before I was born.

I don't even know if your blue eyes
are my blue eyes;
your Swedish ancestors mine,
your DNA mine.
I don't know anything for sure, since the letters—
the ones from Mother's voice teacher.

Does it matter
that a teacher writes his pupil,
or that he calls her "Dearest"?
Does it matter
that he mentions my name saying
he, she, and I could "go away together"?
Does it matter
that he wrote it just days after I was born?

And the gas stove.
The day Mother held me there
in front of its open oven door—
a Kafka-esque, postpartum plan gone awry—
only by chance interrupted by a family member.
Does it still matter?

Now that you are gone—all three—
and have taken this maddening secret with you,
I want to claw at the earth over your grave
to find some reassurance, some DNA—
something of you, matching something of me.

So, Father, does it matter?
More importantly,
would you love me any less
if I told you that it did?

Two Mothers

I had two mothers—two mothers I claim;
two different people, yet with the same name.
Two separate women, diverse by design,
but I loved them both for they were both mine.

The first was the mother who carried me here;
gave birth, nurtured, and launched my career.
She was the woman whose features I bear,
complete with the facial expressions I wear.

She gave me love, which follows me yet,
along with examples in life which she set.
As I became older, she some younger grew,
and we'd laugh just as mothers and daughters can do.

But then came the year that her mind clouded so
and it seemed that the mother I'd known soon would go.
So quickly she changed and turned into the other—
a stranger who dressed in the clothes of my mother.

Oh, she looked the same then, at least at arm's length,
but she was a child now and I was her strength.
We'd come full circle, we women three—
my mother the first, the second, and me.

So if my own children should reach such a day
when a new mother comes and the old goes away,
I'd ask of them nothing that I wouldn't do—
love *both* of your mothers as *both* have loved you.

Mothers Reflected

I had a sudden vision
of my mother the other day—
I was rushing past a row of stores
when she came, and went away.
It was bittersweet to see her
in the window of that shop—
the reflection was so fleeting
that I almost didn't stop.
Years passed since I had seen her,
and yet here without disguise
were those unmistaken frown lines
and those large and haunting eyes.
I almost said, "How are you?"
and, "How wonderful you're here!"
but before I had a chance to speak,
she began to disappear
and the window glass got cloudy
but I'd just time to define
that *I* had become my mother
and that face I'd seen, was *mine.*

So I walked away the wiser,
and I couldn't help but smile,
for I thought I'd lost my mother
yet *she'd been here all the while.*

The Visit

My sister and I were both jittery as we boarded the plane. This was not to be one of those Florida fun-in-the-sun vacations—we were going to see our oldest sister for the last time.

Veronica was the feisty member of our family, with strong opinions about what she wanted and what she didn't—the medical profession fit into the latter. Except for when she gave birth to her five children, and having a broken wrist or two, she stayed clear of doctors and never had any of the diagnostic tests that the rest of us schedule each year. Luckily for her, she had 85 relatively disease-free years before colon cancer struck. Now, two years later, it was back.

Our brother and his wife picked us up at the airport, and as we neared Veronica's double-wide mobile home I remembered how incensed she would be whenever I referred to it as a trailer. "It's a COACH!" she'd insist. We arrived to find her curled up in her bed, looking nothing like the sister we knew—the gallivanting matriarch of the family who, up until two years ago, would get into her car and head up to New England at a moment's notice. As long as she had her tapes of Sinatra and Dorsey on board, she would sing and hum her way across the miles with no problem. It took just one look at that once robust, now pencil thin, body to know that those driving days would be no more.

Though on pain medication, her mind was still quite sharp. She knew what remedies she was to take and when—and let us know it in no uncertain terms. It was the old Veronica shining through the pain.

That afternoon, while she rested in her bedroom, we gathered in the living room, near her absolute favorite possession, a huge state-of-the-art electric organ. Thinking she might enjoy hearing some music, I decided to try my hand at playing the thing, but since its console resembled the cockpit of a plane, I couldn't even find how to turn it on. Soon everyone was looking for the "on" switch, but to no avail.

Suddenly from her bedroom came a very disgusted but determined voice, "Oh, for God's sake—what's the matter with you all!" Evidently she'd heard us discussing the organ dilemma, so down the hall she came, our wisp of a sister, with her now too-big nightie swirling around her too-thin body, but with determination in her eyes.

Then came the magic moment of our whole visit. To our surprise, she not only turned on the organ, but climbed up on that bench and began to play show tunes and old favorites with gusto. My sister Jean, brother Sky, and I commenced to harmonize just the way we did when we were growing up, with our mother playing the piano and father making certain we each stayed on our own part. We four siblings had not been together under the same roof for almost twenty years, and now here we were in this familiar pose, singing our hearts out through our tears.

This would be the last time Veronica played that organ, yet as her body became weaker, her mind still clung to hope. On the day we left for home the phone rang—it was a man from her poker club. To our amazement we heard her tell him in a rather perky voice, "I hope to make it on Wednesday night!"

Eight days later Veronica died in her sleep. No more knitting with what she irreverently called her "stitch and bitch" club, nor entertaining those poker players. No more trips out for breakfast where this otherwise generous soul was famous for finding the cheapest cup of coffee in town. But more importantly, no more pain.

Our round trip tickets to Florida cost $600, but the hours spent with Veronica? Priceless. I just wish you could have heard her play that organ.

VII. Just for Fun

There's a Possum on our Porch

There's a possum on our porch
and we don't know what to do.
We could ask it in for tea
or tell the thing to shoo.

We could sic the terrier on him
but that wouldn't work—we tried—
for the weird thing about possums
is you can't tell if they died.

In Defense of Rhyme

I rhyme! I rhyme!
And though it's thought a crime,
I love to hear things sound alike
so I rhyme from time to time.

I do it in the coffee shop,
I do it in the park,
and sometimes when I'm frantic
I do it in the dark!

I do it when I'm happy,
I do it when I'm sad,
I like to do so much of it
I fear I might go mad.

Rhyme did okay for Shakespeare,
it rang the bell for Poe,
and what about Emily Dickinson
with matched metaphors all in a row?

I'm happy to plead guilty,
prepared to do my time,
so lock me up in some dank, dark cell—
I'll have **lots** of time to rhyme!

Larry the Plumber

Larry the plumber was priceless—
a hilarious sort, through and through.
He'd regale all the guys at the diner
with tales not just funny, but *true*!
The best one of all dealt with Gladys
who called in a panic one day
screaming, *"Larry, you've got to get up here—
the seat on my throne just gave way!"*

"No problem!" said Larry, "I'm comin'!"
He went up there, right after she called.
He measured, then left, and returned again
and a new seat was duly installed.
That night came a phone call from Gladys—
"Oh Larry, it just doesn't fit!"
Again came, "No problem!" from Larry—
he got a new one, and then installed IT!

But that's not the end of the story—
from Gladys came call after call.
"Only one way to please her," said Larry,
"I'd fix this thing once and for all!
I bought me a big piece of cardboard
and a wide magic marker," said he,
"and headed my truck back to Gladys—
I'd end this seat saga, by Gee!"

"I said, Gladys, I've got the solution—
no longer will this thing confound ya!
Sit down on this-here piece of cardboard
and I'm going to trace all around ya!"

And he did.

Grave Upgrade

They've been widening Route 33
from Greenland to Portsmouth,
slicing dangerously close
to graves lining the perimeter
of Calvary Cemetery.

I hope I'm not driving
over somebody's toes.

A Pantihose Dilemma

Pity the poor pantihose,
in such a constant snit—
not knowing if they're plural
or are they just an "it."

One panty—sure, that's obvious—
but the stockings? More than one.
Living in their hybrid world's
not their idea of fun.

And not easy for the shopper—
what's a poor girl to do?
If she purchases a pair of these,
will she get just *one* or *two*?

So good luck, you struggling pantihose,
in solving your dilemma,
and one day may you finally know
if you're a "this-a" or a "them-a."

At the Dentist's

It is May of my 26th year.
I am sitting in a dentist chair
in downtown Malden, Massachusetts,
about to be separated from three wisdom teeth,
and worrying about my brain capacity
once they're gone.
Meanwhile, down below in the Town Square
I hear Torbet MacDonald, a political candidate,
revving up his constituents, as they wave their placards
and cheer in loud, adoring response.

Now, enter Dr. G., a man previously unknown to me.
I smile, unaware that I am about to experience
something bordering on the bizarre.
The moment the Novacaine begins to do his bidding,
Dr. G. picks up the first of many instruments
and commences to sing loudly and incessantly—
as if a magic line is strung from his vocal cords
to his busily maneuvering hands.
He then bellows forth with gusto
a nonending repertoire from Rossini's "Figaro"
to Sinatra's "All The Way,"
with hardly a breath in between.

I sit frozen in the chair
as the yanking grows harder and harder
and the music, louder and louder—
a sort of Ravel's "Bolero"
set to an extraction theme.

Finally, at the end of that day,
I had lost three wisdom teeth,
Torbet MacDonald headed for
victory in the election,
and Dr. G. made straight
for his bottle of gargle elixir
in preparation for his next patient
who sat in the waiting room
unaware of what was about to transpire.

I could only hope—
for this poor man's sake—
that he was a devotee of musical theater.

Diamonds on Diamonds

First, the eyes of everyone there
were on those gorgeous, dazzling earrings.
Diamonds—not zirconium and certainly not glass—
but the real thing,
and the afternoon sun was reflecting off
their every single chiseled facet.

And next, that necklace—
thick links of pure satiny gold.
Had to be 24 karats and nothing less,
and exuding an air of elegance
and high fashion for all to see.

Then finally, a cheer went up
as the object of our attention
took his place on the mound
and threw the first pitch of the game.

Major league ball players
just don't dress the way they used to.

Recycling, Anyone?

At our town's recycling center
they've now developed the art
of giving all sorts of our clutter
a new chance at life—a new start!

While great for our paper and plastic,
and earth-wise a definite plus,
how come they haven't discovered
a method to recycle *us*?

Ellie McNelly

(*This fanciful verse was a Facebook experiment: I posted two lines, then asked for volunteers to add their own, to see where the poem would go. Soon, poet friends Bob Moore and Janet Fipphen jumped in here and there with their imaginations in tow. Here is what happened to Ellie McNelly.*)

Ellie McNelly flew off to the mall
in search of some new things to wear.
The shoes she admired were six inches tall—
they seemed an adventurous pair.
But Ellie McNelly looked tall as a tree
and that wouldn't do, so instead
she kicked off her shoes and her socks and then thought
to buy flowery wreaths for her head.

This halo of flowers had magical powers,
and swooped her twelve feet in the air.
She flew and she flew—and I swear this is true—
'til she landed in Amherst's town square.
She stood up to wonder what spell she was under;
what flowers have powers so strange?
Not daisies, not posies, but tiny red rosies—
the kind you'd not find on the range.

Then when the air shifted, the flowers uplifted
her over to Emily's house
where dear Ms. Dickinson, calling the chickens in,
slipped as she tripped on a mouse.
Said Emmy to Ellie, "*I hope you'll excuse me,
my white gown is now a light brown.*"
"Take one of my flowers with their magical powers,
and your gown will be whiter than down."

Then Ellie McNelly and Emily D.
conversed by the fire's slant of light.
They wrote a few poems and six palindro-ems
but something was clearly not right—
that halo of rosies on Ellie's small head
started whirring and blinking and steaming!
The next thing she knew she was home in her bed—
it turns out that Ellie'd been dreaming!

Now this three-authored verse, for better or worse,
has inched its fine way to an end—
which all goes to show, what by now you may know—
it's *sublime* when you *rhyme* with a friend!

A Tale of Three Tubs

Tub #1. My friend Edna and her husband Randy were in Paris, and had just checked into their hotel when Edna decided she would treat herself to a long, luxurious bath in their suite's inviting tub. She made the most of it, she said, going heavy on the complimentary bubble bath and settling in for a long, welcome soak.

When the water finally cooled and she tried to alight from the tub, however, she realized she had a problem: before getting in, she neglected to take measurements of the tub's width in relation to her own. Now, all that warm water had plumped up her skin enough to lock her ample hips to the unforgiving sides of that tub. She immediately called to Randy for help, and back came a reply she didn't want to hear. "Sorry, I've already gone to bed and I've taken my leg off." Randy, you see, had a prosthetic limb, and putting it back on was not an easy task, but he told her he'd see that she got out. Soon, two burly men came up from the Front Desk, flung open the bathroom door and announced that they were going to extricate her from the tub, and after some tugging and pulling, they did. Though highly embarrassed, Edna forgave Randy, but my playful mind still can't help wondering whether Randy actually *had* already taken his prosthesis off that night when she called for help.

Tub #2. My mother had a friend, Mrs. Locke, who often came to visit. She was close to ninety years old and lived in a house that had no bathtub. Mother always thought that was a real shame, so one day during Mrs. Locke's visit, she up and asked her if she wouldn't like to take a bath in our tub. It was an outrageous question, but evidently it hit the spot and Mrs. Locke said she would. Mother got things ready for her, gave her some assistance into the tub and left her there, content with the warm afternoon sun shining in on one happy woman basking in suds. When Mrs. Locke left that day, she thanked my mother profusely for her wonderful bath—the first she'd had in years.

The next morning the phone rang and it was Mrs. Locke's son. "Mother died in her sleep last night— thought you would want to know." For years, my mother suffered pangs of guilt, certain that she'd done Mrs. Locke in with that bath, but took some solace in the knowledge that she went to her reward squeaky clean.

Tub #3. Unlike the others, this tub had not one drop of water in it, but did provide a lesson that could come in handy for the rest of us some day. My friend Marion's husband Harry had been ailing for some time, and it became difficult for him to get around. Occasionally he would fall, and since he weighed much more than Marion, they would have to call 911 for assistance in righting Harry. It embarrassed them to think they had to bother the firemen and policemen so often. Then one night Marion heard a frantic call from the upstairs bathroom. Somehow Harry had lost his balance and fell into the empty tub, but didn't have the strength to hoist himself up.

Determined not to bother 911 again, the couple began to brainstorm for an alternate way of at least boosting Harry up a bit until he could climb out himself. Since Marion is quite a reader, books came to mind, and she hurried downstairs and returned with a good-sized one which she pushed and maneuvered under Harry's backside. Unfortunately, one book fell short, so Marion went down and got another, again tucking it under Harry. Still not high enough. This went on for many trips to the downstairs bookcase until finally Harry was able to pull himself up and out of the tub. Yankee ingenuity triumphed.

So there are the tales of three tub dilemmas: the first solved by two burly strangers; the second solved by my mother, but ending in death; and the third proving you can never underestimate the power of a good book.

VIII. On the
Serious Side

Rolling Home

From birth to death
we bobble along
on life's conveyor belt
like so many hapless confections
at the chocolate factory,

except
in our case,

there is no Lucille Ball
to catch us
at the end.

A Modest Star

—In memory of Wally Newton

When such a modest star goes out
and vanishes from sight,
it has no thought of how its loss
could dim the velvet night.
Quite unassuming, somewhat shy,
it lived life unaware
of what a brilliant light it gave
or that the world would care.

Yet those who saw it, felt its love,
touched by its humble ways,
will never view a midnight sky
without a word of praise
for the quiet star that shone there
so silent, yet so tall,
that even now, with flame gone out,
it glows here, in us all.

Tap Dancing on Tissue Paper

As age climbs and remaining years dwindle,
we think about life—the uncertainty of it all.
We read the daily news and find ourselves
whistling by the graveyard—we are all
tap dancing on tissue paper.

Newly retired George Anderson, 62,
disappears while on anniversary cruise.
  Tappity—TAP!

Theresa Grignafini, age 68, crashes vehicle
through pharmacy window.
  Tappity—tappity—TAP!

Marathon runner Ernestine Wallace, 70,
dies unexpectedly during gall bladder surgery.
  Tappity—tappity—tappity—TAP!

Research shows the majority of breast cancers
are found in older women.
  Tappity—tappity—tappity—tappity—TAP!

*An estimated 4.5 million Americans
have Alzheimer's Disease.*

Tappity—tappity—tappity—tappity—tappity—
tappity—tappity—tappity—tappity—tappity—
tappity—tappity—tappity—tappity—tappity—
tappity—tappity—tappity—tappity—tappity—
tappity—tappity—tappity—tappity—tappity—
tappity—tappity—tappity—tappity—tappity—
tappity—tappity—tappity . . .

Whither?

We come, we go,
they come, they go,
everyone comes, everyone goes,
but in the end,
no one seems to know
just where.

Someday there will be
a microchip
for the soul.

No Postcards from Heaven

—In memory of Rev. Dick Duncanson

How long should I wait, do you suppose?
You'd think I'd have heard from you
by now.

All these years since your body and soul
went their separate ways
leaving me a road map to just one,
yet I've heard nothing.

No need for an essay or sonnet,
or even a brief haiku.
Just something—a card, a note:
"Having spiritual time, wish you were here."

It's strange, I know, but tomorrow
I will go to my mailbox once again
looking for a sign, anything,
even though deep down, I know—
as I have always known—
there are no postcards from heaven.

Boxes

I have these boxes—
not real boxes, but boxes in the mind.

There is a large, sturdy box with a tight-fitting lid
for those unwanted thoughts and fears
that come in the night,
tearing through the covers of my bed and mind—
warning me of things that may, or may never,
come to be.

There is an old dust-covered box
for repressed memories—
child birthing pain,
a young husband's death,
a mother's indiscretion.

There is a long thin box
for old unyielding grudges
that chafe and persist for years.

There is a tall black box
for abortions of the mind—
poems yet unfinished,
essays in utero,
songs still unsung.

There is a colorful, whimsical box
with no cover at all,
for dreams yet to come true
and ideas yet to be born.

And finally,
just one tiny round box
for tears.
Tears should never
require much room.

These are my boxes.

Sometimes I think of them
and wonder just what I shall do
when they are all filled.

Disconnect

God and I
are not on good speaking terms.

We don't call—we never write.

In fact, you might say
we were never even
properly introduced.

Church Lament

I wouldn't mind
if I never entered a church again,
if it weren't for *the people*—
that way they have of greeting you
flesh to flesh, eye to eye, heart to heart,
         or
if it weren't for *the caring*—
feeding the hungry, tending the sick,
tucking themselves in around the bereaved
like soft woolen blankets,
         or
if it weren't for *the music*—
that tide of Amazing Grace
dancing over chancels,
swirling under pews,
until finally coming to rest
in our souls themselves.

Wouldn't it be ironic
for doubters like me
who struggle to put a
face on a deity,
if these three things—
the people,
the caring,
the music—
were God?

Lower Me Gently

Lower me gently,
scatter me free—
these are my wishes
for what's left of me.

Bone weight or feather,
either will do—
no one is home now,
no one you knew.

Instead, I grow weightless,
I've shed my earth's case
and no longer need
to put powder to face.

Now you may find me
on beams of the moon,
or circling a cup's rim
in late afternoon.

Or tucked in a sweater
between knit and purl—
or on a cat's whisker,
or the blush of a girl.

So, trowel or wind gust—
each of them kind.
Do what you will now,
I'll never mind.

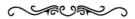

What to Leave Behind
When the End Comes

That bumper sticker saying, *I'm spending my children's inheritance,* came to mind one day while visiting some retired friends up north. They were telling of their recent trip to England and another they have planned for the Fall, along with a few other expensive jaunts in the offing. Now, I've known this couple for forty years and they have never been even remotely mistaken for spendthrifts; they live conservatively. When retirement came, they opted for a modest manufactured home—the kind that comes down the highway in two pieces with the vehicle carrying the WIDE LOAD sign just ahead of them. It has served their purposes well and they've been spending their retirement there ever since—happily but frugally. That's why this last conversation with them came as somewhat of a surprise.

"Goodness," I said, "all these trips make it sound as if you two have either overdosed on Geritol or hit the lottery. What happened?"

"Well," they replied, "one of our sons is now in charge of international taxation for one of the largest companies in the northeast—and the other is a corporate attorney for a huge telecommunications firm. We finally came to the realization that these boys and their families can now shift for themselves—they don't need our financial help. We don't have to scrimp and save for them any more—we're not getting any younger."

Many retired parents still have this dilemma, however. They worry that their children may need financial help, so they feel it is their sacred duty to live meagerly in order to leave as much money behind as possible. They live out their lives on a financial see-saw, with their own comforts and needs on one end and the possible needs of their maturing kids on the other.

Deciding how much money to spend and how much to save in retirement is not an easy matter because the decision depends on how long you have to live, and therein lies the rub. If our bodies came with shelf dates stamped on them the way cartons of milk do, retirement planning would be a lot easier.

There is no reason for conjecture in our family when it comes to who inherits what when I go. My two children are the best things that ever happened to me, but they know that given my almost nonexistent financial portfolio, there'll be no need to hire a Brinks' truck to carry the inheritance from my bank to theirs; when my time comes, a tiny Matchbox car will probably do the trick.

That old adage about parents giving children roots and wings still seems to make sense. We provide them with a good foundation, then later on they take flight to make their own way in life. Of course, some of them learn to fly better than others, while a few simply never get to take off at all. These are the exceptions—the ones who never outgrow their need for parental attention and money. Mom, Dad, or both, answer their distress calls, giving help where they can, even when they know deep inside that continual help, though given in love, may in the long run not be help at all.

Multimillionaire Warren Buffett has it right with his plans to leave only a portion of his fortune to his children. He says he believes in leaving them just enough money so they can do *something,* but not so much that they will do *nothing.*

I can't help wondering, however, just what Mr. Buffett means by *something.*

IX. A Postcript
for Poets

Sandboxes

All I know is this:
we poets are either
in this world
or *of* it—
but we cannot be both.

We are anomalies—
misfits of a sort—
our minds play in
different sandboxes;
theirs filled with sand,
ours with
fragments of dreams,
grains of possibilities,
particles of rhyme.

Even when we leave
our boxes, tiny remnants
of meter and metaphor
cling fiercely to the soles
of our sandals
reminding us that
we can be either
in this world
or *of* it,
but it is often
so very difficult
to be both.

A Poet's Two Worlds

Living in two worlds divides the soul—
one portion going here, the other there.
I envy those whose lives make up a whole—
they stay one course, and never two compare.

They know when they arise what they must do—
what role to play, what costume to put on.
They do just what the world has asked them to,
and welcome so predictable a dawn.

The rest of us were made from different clay—
we live divided, tortured in the brain—
and always there's that voice so far away
that pulls us there, while we must here remain.

So—we live on with prose and poetry
packed side by side within our weary bones,
yet we may never be completely free
until just *one* is mentioned on our stones.

Go Little Poems, Go!

From a twinkle in my heart
I conceived you
shaped you
embellished you
nurtured you
watched you grow
until now,
when I have done
all that can be done.

You have earned your wings
so go out into the world—
go little poems, go.

Now get out of here, will you?!